ISBN 978-0-9566233-0-0

Published by Abhann Productions Limited
(with thanks to Rein Gerlofs for his assistance)

Printed in Northern Ireland by W&G Baird (www.wgbaird.com)

Production management: Rein Gerlofs, Patricia Carroll & Deborah Gilmartin
Editor: Sinéad Clandillon
Artwork: Klaas Greydanus & Nicole McKenna

Visit us at www.riverdance.com

Composed by
BILL WHELAN

Produced by
MOYA DOHERTY

Directed by
JOHN McCOLGAN

THE IRISH MUSIC & DANCE PHENOMENON

This is the story of **Riverdance** starting from its early beginnings in 1994, to a show that is now celebrated and loved around the world. Its journey is documented in this book through stunning images, which capture the beauty, energy, excitement and joy of the live shows at its many performances across the globe.

'The original...the best'
The Irish Times

'Triumphant! A perfect gem! ... An entertainment mammoth!
New York Post

Riverdance

COMPOSED BY BILL WHELAN
PRODUCED BY MOYA DOHERTY
DIRECTED BY JOHN McCOLGAN

Of all the performances to emerge from Ireland in the past decade – in rock, music, theatre and film – nothing has carried the energy, the sensuality and the spectacle of **Riverdance.**

Since **Riverdance** began performances in Dublin 1995, the show has been seen live by over 22 million people in over 300 venues worldwide, throughout 32 countries across 4 continents. Over 10 million videos and DVDs have been sold and Bill Whelan's **Riverdance** CD won a Grammy Award for Best Musical Show Album in 1997.

'The phenomenon rolls on!...
There will always be a **Riverdance**!'
New York Times, March 2000

Contents

RIVERDANCE, Act 2

HARBOUR OF THE NEW WORLD

A NEW DIRECTION IN IRISH DANCE

THE HEART OF RIVERDANCE

REFLECTIONS

Denise Whelan, Bill Whelan, Moya Doherty and John McColgan at the opening of *Riverdance* On Broadway at the Gershwin Theatre, March 2000

BILL WHELAN
COMPOSER

Sixteen years have elapsed since Moya Doherty and I sat in a coffee shop in Baggot Street, Dublin and imagined what was to become the centrepiece of Eurovision 1994. Those years have been so crammed with incident, so full of extraordinary memories that it is almost impossible to write briefly about them without doing them rank injustice. So much has changed in that time. Globally, we have seen massive shifts and the arrival of new uncertainties. In Ireland, we have witnessed unprecedented economic and social change, peace on the island, and a whole range of new possibilities and challenges.

When our *Riverdance* gospel choir sang in Donnybrook Church in 1995, they were somewhat of a curiosity. Now, gospel choirs can be heard in many places throughout Ireland, and Eastern European musicians are not the rarity they were in the Point Theatre when we opened the show. The concept of *Riverdance* – where a native culture goes out and brings back influences to the homeplace – is now being replayed by other cultures here among us in Ireland. And so the river flows….

The big events will always be moments to cherish. The first night in Dublin, the London opening, Radio City Music Hall, Broadway, the night at the Grammys, the Special Olympics, China – they will be ever there for those of us who were involved. But sometimes it is the personal details that we cherish. For me, watching Johnny McDonagh explain the subtleties of the bodhrán to Crown Prince Naruhito of Japan will always give me a smile. Or being told by a massive African American gentleman in Georgia that his daughter danced to *Riverdance* music every night. These little anecdotal details often really tell the story of the extraordinary reach of this show that we have all been so fortunate to have been part of. •

MOYA DOHERTY
PRODUCER

Where did those years go? How did they pass so swiftly while the heartbeat of *Riverdance* pulsed confidently around the world, feet pounding the earth like a drum?

To sit and ponder the passage of time is to allow a wash of extraordinary, unbelievable, funny, joyous, sad memories flow through the memory bank. It's impossible to separate the personal, the professional, the universal, all intrinsically intertwined. One thing is certain, I am fifteen years older, I moved from my thirties to my fifties, my young sons grew to be men, my parents passed away, Ireland changed dramatically.

John, the Director, in his reflection celebrates the commitment of the performers one and all. As Producer I am drawn to reflect on the dedication and commitment of the back-room men and women, whose history with the show is as long as my own.

Dangerous to name names but maturity has given me the confidence to be bold.

Thank you to:
Maurice Cassidy, the promoter of dreams
Julian Erskine, the manager of dreams
Clint Mitchell, the agent of dreams
Merle Frimark and Gerry Lundberg, the sellers of dreams
Joan Egan, the minder of dreams

And the creative quartet:
Joan Bergin, the weaver of dreams
Robert Ballagh, the painter of dreams
Mick O'Gorman, the sound of dreams
and dear Rupert Murray, whom we miss very much, shone light on dreams and into all our lives.

Riverdance has been a true journey of collaboration and friendship. •

JOHN McCOLGAN
DIRECTOR

So many shows, so many memories, so much pride.
For fifteen years I have stood in darkened theatres and arenas all over the world watching *Riverdance* on stage – from the first unforgettable show at the Point Theatre in Dublin, on to London, New York, Germany, China, Japan, Mexico, hundreds of cities around the world. Every performance and every night the same rapturous response.

Today, the touring shows are as fresh and potent as ever, given new life every night by hundreds of committed dancers, singers, musicians. Their belief in ***Riverdance***, their pride and professionalism, the love of their work shines from the stage entrancing and capturing the hearts of their audience.

These Irish and international performers continue to be a vibrant expression of a modern multicultural Ireland, reflecting our new-found sense of confidence in who we are, in what we represent: a country with a deep-rooted and rich heritage, proud of our past, confident in our future, an island at peace.

I am proud of these performers and as I watch from the dark I continue to be in awe of their commitment and ability – every night giving their all to create the magic that is ***Riverdance***. •

REEL AROUND THE SUN

In a primitive and powerful world, our ancestors knew fear and joy and fire, worked wood and stone and water to make a place they could call home. The first peoples knew the world as a place of power. Their songs and dances and stories are negotiations with elemental powers. The first half of this performance shows them coming to terms with the world and with themselves.

The sun brings life and light and fire, the opening dance sequence celebrates this benevolent masculine power. The sun is the light of morning, exuberant and clear. •

Out of the dark we came
Out of the sea
Where the long wave broke
on the shore
As the day broke
And the night rolled back
There we stood on the land
We would call home

Poetry: Theo Dorgan

THE HEART'S CRY

There is also that other primeval mystery, the salmon swimming upstream, the blind impulse of nature, heart yearning to heart. We need and sustain each other; we keep this knowledge in song since the beginning of time. •

Where the river foams and surges to the sea
Silver figures rise to find me
Wise and as daring
Following the heart's cry
I am that deep pool
I am that dark spring
Warm with a mystery
I may reveal to you

Lyrics: Bill Whelan

THE COUNTESS CATHLEEN
WOMEN OF THE SIDHE

Sensual, nurturing, independent and fierce, the power of women as they celebrate themselves, as they challenge men in a dance of empowerment. •

24

BEYOND WORDS
THE STORY OF RIVERDANCE

BY FINTAN O'TOOLE

When **Riverdance** first opened in Dublin, you could hear, even above the pounding feet and the swirling music, the audience gasping for breath. And then an explosion of shouts and whoops as all that air burst out again in a wave of wonderment. It was, of course, the sheer force and energy of the dancing, the rapture of the music, the fantastic sight of so many bodies in motion. But there was something else as well, some long-submerged emotion breaking the surface and gulping in the oxygen.

Overnight sensations seldom last. In the merciless world of show business, today's novelty becomes old news in the blinking of an eye. No amount of hype or clever marketing can sustain a show beyond its immediate impact. Unless, that is, it is fuelled by some deeper source of energy. And it can't just draw from that source. It also has to renew it, to give back at least as much as it has taken. **Riverdance** has continued to find and excite audiences all around the world because it does both of these things. Even as it grows and changes, it stays in touch with the emotions that made that opening night audience gasp. Even as it touches people in distant places, it continues to shape and refresh the culture from which it sprang.

Traditional dancing starts out as an expression of togetherness. It conveys a sense of belonging. Everyone knows the steps. Everyone can join in. The different generations and classes become, while the dance goes on, part of a community. It depends, therefore, on the existence of a stable culture. The moves, the rhythms and the patterns are passed down from generation to generation. However lively the movements, however wild the rhythms, there is, behind them, a quiet confidence that this community will always exist, that these rituals will always celebrate its survival.

But, of course, the communities don't just survive, they change. New influences come in. People move from the country to the city. And, in the case of Ireland over the last two centuries, they move from their own country to foreign cities. They take their music, their dances, their stories with them. And those things no longer say what they used to. They no longer express a stable, familiar world. The ears have to tune in to new sounds. The feet have to move to new, and at first strange, rhythms. The stories have to connect with new experiences. These things have happened to all traditional cultures in one form or another. As the world shrinks, as technology impinges on everything, as closed societies are opened up, everything gets mixed up. All cultures face the same questions: How do we relate to the past? What does the culture we inherited from our ancestors mean now that the world that shaped it is slipping away?

People are faced with an unhappy choice. They can try to preserve their traditional culture by putting up barriers against the outside world and trying to resist change. Or they can go with the flow, forget the past and melt into a bland, generic culture where everything is the same and nothing has much depth. One way leads to isolation and hostility. The other to a nagging sense of loss. But there is another possibility. It is to carry what you have taken from the past on an open-ended journey, showing it off, throwing it open, making it into a point of contact rather than a point of honour. This is what **Riverdance** has done.

It's not, of course, the first Irish show to reach out to international audiences. But it undertakes its journey with the great advantages of dance. Dancers are metaphorically as well as literally light on their feet. They carry less baggage than other performers do. Their language of steps and movements doesn't need translation. The materials they work with – feet, legs, arms, heads – are pretty much the same in every part of the world. Their response to the infectious music may be more complex, more elegant, more athletic than the toes tapping in the audience, but it comes from the same timeless and natural urge.

What the first audiences saw in Dublin and what made them gasp, was that the movement in **Riverdance** reflects the dynamic way in which Irish culture has actually evolved. It has always been about fusions and adaptations, as new impulses are absorbed into the old frameworks and old ideas that seemed to be buried, suddenly re-emerge with a new meaning and a new urgency. But it was always hard to capture this ebb and flow in performance. Things had to be either traditional or modern, either authentic or invented, either Irish or foreign. And then with one elegant, confident leap, **Riverdance** bounded over all those categories and expressed what Irish people have always felt – that you can have it both ways. You can honour the past best by giving it a future. You can preserve a tradition only by letting it live, breathe and change.

And the real proof of all of this is that **Riverdance** has re-energised the tradition from which it springs. Bad commercial shows exploit the forms and feelings they make use of, finally sucking them dry. **Riverdance**, on the contrary, has watered the roots of Irish dancing. It has created a previously unimaginable excitement, drawing in a new generation, releasing new energies, opening up new possibilities. And in turn, these forces have fed back into the show itself. Young dancers enthused by **Riverdance** when it first appeared are now taking their places in the thunderous chorus. For them, **Riverdance** is already part of the best tradition of all – the tradition of making old things new. •

CAOINEADH CHÚ CHULAINN

A lone piper mourns Chú Chulainn, the implacable Bronze Age warrior, the great hero of Celtic myth. •

Chú Chulainn is dead
Our great Chú Chulainn
He was a shield of bronze
A wall of stone
He was a spear of light
A watcher in high places
A rock in the river
He was the sun of morning
He was a fire at night
He was a powerful story
He was lightning in forest
A sudden storm
A short life

Poetry: Theo Dorgan

THUNDERSTORM

The brute power of elemental forces, beyond human control, beyond human understanding. •

Thunder and lightning
batter the rocks
The winds howl and great
storms break on the forest
Scatter the herds like grain
Fire leaps from dark to dark
Fear and anger leap to meet it
We will not go down
We will not be beaten down
like grain

Poetry: Theo Dorgan

36

SHIVNA

The myth of Mad Sweeney, Suibhne or Shivna, haunts Ireland since medieval times. Driven by forces inside of himself, outside himself, a man dances desperately in the power of the moon. The powers are cruel and arbitrary, otherwordly and savage. •

A Bhennáin, a bhúiredáin, a bhéicedáin bhinn
Is bhinn linn in cúicherán do ní tú 'sin ghlinn

A dhraighnéin, a dhelgnacháin
(dil, dol, doh, roh day)
A mhinéin na chonaire
(dil, dol, doh, ray)
A dhriséoc, a dhruimnechóc
(dil, dol, doh, roh day)
A chaillech, a chuirrechennach in raga for ech?

Lyrics from the Ulster cycle poem,
"Suibhne Geilt'"

40

FIREDANCE

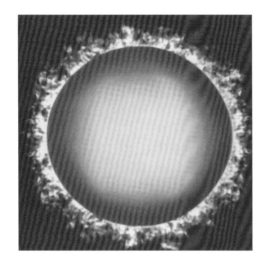

In ancient Ireland fire and pride and beauty come out of the south, from the land of the sun. The power of the sun invests itself in the passion of the dancer. •

RIVERDANCE – THE MUSIC

BY BILL WHELAN

There are two particular problems for the composer writing music in the idiom of any given folk or ethnic tradition – one is social and the other is technical. If the composer is Irish and working with the modes and forms of traditional Irish music, then the first of these problems is most acute – and for very positive reasons.

Traditional music holds a special position in Ireland. To many Irish people it has a defining role culturally and provides an authentic and eloquent link to their past. It is also a rich musical vein that reveals much about Ireland and the Irish – quirky, mischievous, evasive dance tunes, and dark proud airs that can heal grief and comfort loss.

So, when you find yourself in and around a music that has such a long tradition, and such delicate associations and nuance, it can begin to feel like being in a church. Even the lightest footfall can echo long and you may think twice before you dare to whisper.

From a technical point of view, the instruments from which this music has grown are themselves problematic. In particular the uilleann pipes, not being chromatic, tend to confine melodic writing and the very nature of the instrument itself demands caution. The uilleann pipes are a very beautiful but frustrating combination. Both primitive and sophisticated, their evocative abilities are boundless, but the piper's terror is that they may decide to desert him in the midst of his most ardent flight, like some haughty lover – sweet, mysterious and unpredictable. This dynamic goes to the heart of piping and the composer may do well to remember the piper's careful pampering of his reeds before setting a note on the page.

Add to this the varied demands created by whistles, bodhráns, Irish fiddling styles, and in the case of **Riverdance**, the quirks and vagaries of the Eastern gadulkas and kavals, and soon the relative familiarity of a symphony orchestra may beckon like a safe harbour in a storm.

In such conditions one might never venture out the door. Even ignoring the technical constraints, the social imperatives are daunting enough. However, it is a testament to the robust state of Irish traditional music at this time, that there is enough confidence abroad to allow for innovation. While the tradition stands firm, modes of expression are changing and in the broad new church of Irish music, one may now dare to whisper – even to sing.

I have said much about the process of writing for and working with the kinds of musical ingredients that I had chosen for **Riverdance**. However, composition is essentially a solitary occupation, and it is only when you first bring your music into the dance studio that you experience the full rush of fear and excitement. The dancers are not quite prepared for what to expect, and you have no idea how they are going to respond.

It would be folly to suggest that we all knew exactly what we were at, or that there was some kind of grand design. But there is no doubt that as the pieces began to fit together, there was a sense that something unique was happening around and among us. I had deliberately written pieces with rhythmic patterns that were foreign to traditional Irish music, but after the initial raised eyebrows the thrust of the principal dancers' creativity took hold and I can still remember the excitement as they began to fashion their first steps.

Gradually these steps were learnt by the troupe and I have many memories of arriving to the studio to find individual dancers in corners, corridors and canteens as they worked on the kind of precision that was to become a hallmark of **Riverdance**.

And then came the day that, for me, really copper-fastened it. It was one of the last days of rehearsal for the Eurovision in 1994. Producer Moya Doherty, myself and the entire company were assembled in the dance studio. There was hardly room to move. We had seen the dance performed in sections, but had not seen it all in one piece. The music began, and for the next six minutes the room was like a power-station. When it was over we all just looked at each other and smiled. There may have been no grand design, but we knew at that moment that whatever it was, it worked. **Riverdance** was truly on its feet and I will never forget it. •

SLIP INTO SPRING – THE HARVEST

The wheel of the seasons turns slowly, from harvest through dormant winter into the miracle of spring. New growth, exhilaration, the world turns and is made new again. •

RIVERDANCE
RIVERDANCE TRACES THE LIFE OF A RIVER

The invocation sung at the start is called Cloudsong: it is the rain falling, feeding the river, which springs to life and flows through the land and out to sea. There, the cloud reforms and returns to the land, nourishing, renewing and refreshing it. The constant refrain 'uisce beatha' translates as 'water of life'. The number builds from the gentle song to the dancers' feet rhythmically recalling a river gathering force and rushing to the sea. The choreography reflects this cycle. The riverwoman dances alone, her soft-shoe dance evoking the flow of the river. As she crosses the land, the earth, represented by the male dancer, awakens and bursts forth onto the stage. As the strength of the river builds, so dancers gather, signifying new life and energy, until the full **Riverdance** line swells to fill the stage as the river meets the sea. Then earth and river dance in harmony, as the water of life renews the land.

The river, from cloud to sea to cloud again, symbolises the life cycle, and echoes the Irish experience of emigration and renewal: people who had left their homeland and travelled across the sea, returned in the 1990s to enrich Ireland with their talents and experience gained abroad. The show as a whole builds on this idea, also exploring the way people from different lands enrich the countries they emigrate to, bringing with them their own culture, music and dance. •

CLOUDSONG

Hear my cry
In my hungering search for you
Taste my breath on the wind
See the sky
As it mirrors my colours
Hints and whispers begin

I am living to nourish you, cherish you
I am pulsing the blood in your veins
Feel the magic and power of surrender
To life, Uisce Beatha

Every finger is touching and searching
Until your secrets come out
In the dance, as it endlessly circles
I linger close to your mouth

I am living to nourish you, cherish you
I am pulsing the blood in your veins
Feel the magic and power of surrender
To life, Uisce Beatha

Lyrics: Bill Whelan

52

War, famine and slavery shattered the ancient bonds between people and place. Forced dislocations marked and altered the histories of the native peoples. As we came into history we learned to guard what we valued, to accommodate ourselves to others, to learn new ways of being ourselves, to embrace new kinds of courage. Cast out and momentarily orphaned, we learned to belong to the world.

AMERICAN WAKE

From the mid-19th century, hunger and famine and ambition drove the Irish out of their home island, across the Atlantic to a New World. Lover parted from lover, families and communities were torn apart. •

In dance and song we gift
and mourn our children
They carry us over the ocean
In dance and song

Poetry: Theo Dorgan

Lift the wings that carry me away from here and
fill the sail that breaks the line to home
But when I'm miles and miles apart from you
I'm beside you when I think of you, a Stóirín a ghrá

Lyrics: Bill Whelan

LIFT THE WINGS

While those souls who were forced to
emigrate were faced with the heartbreak of
separation, their human spirit was often lifted
by a defiant hope at the prospect of a new
life. •

HARBOUR OF THE NEW WORLD
HEAL THEIR HEARTS – FREEDOM

From the darkness a lone voice sings and is
then joined by other immigrants, reflecting
the universal yearning of the dispossessed
wherever they make their home.

HEAL THEIR HEARTS

In the deep night
From a dark space
I hear voices calling out in heartache
They are wounded
They are broken
But their spirit rises when awoken
Yes, they may be poor in birth – but
Yes, how great each one is worth

Heal their hearts
Feed their souls
Their lives can be golden
if your love enfolds

Lyrics: Bill Whelan

62

FREEDOM

Lord, where is our freedom?
When will our hope begin?
Lord, what of the promise you made?
When will it come?
We have waited for the time
For the truth to live,
when justice will shine
Too long those hands of greed
Held on and made us bleed
When will your people breathe?
Lord, will it come?

Lyrics: Bill Whelan

TRADING TAPS

The wealth of the poor is in song, dance and story. Under the street-lamps in the new cities, the dancers perform with pride in their heritage, curious to see what other traditions bring, struggling to bridge the gap between old dreams and new realities. ●

Tall and straight
my mother taught me
This is how we dance
Tall and straight
my Father taught me
This is how we dance
Battering feet on the city street
in pools of light on street corners
The proud bright carnival of the poor

Poetry: Theo Dorgan

MORNING IN MACEDONIA/
THE RUSSIAN DERVISH

Meeting the new, what we learn first is that there is something familiar in what is strange, something strange in what we had thought familiar. A tune from another place, another lifetime, can turn and haunt in the heart. •

Over the roof tops the music calling
The air familiar but not our own
Like something out of a story book
Somebody dancing, the memory of snow

Poetry: Theo Dorgan

OSCAIL AN DORAS

In the flight from famine and poverty, musical instruments were an unknown luxury. "Mouth Music" often used by the Celtic nations was now revived as a substitute dance accompaniment and also as relief from the tedium of manual labour. •

ANDALUCÍA

In the cauldron of the big city, the pulsing energy of the streets is reflected in the fiery Latin dance rhythms.

SLOW AIR AND TUNES/ HEARTLAND

Always the child of the emigrant feels the tug of the homeplace; always that child feels the urge to return. What she or he brings there is a sustaining knowledge: we are who we once were, we are who we have become.

With newfound confidence and pride, the child of the emigrant carries treasured memories home to their birthplace. A long journey ends under a native sky, a new and richer journey has taken its place.

And after all
The moon over city and forest
is everywhere the same
In the old land it silvers fields
of grain
Just as it does here
The rivers everywhere run down
to the sea
And the land everywhere takes
life from the river

Poetry: Theo Dorgan

A NEW DIRECTION IN IRISH DANCE

BY JOHN McCOLGAN

From the first performance of **Riverdance** at the 1994 Eurovision Song Contest in Dublin, we knew that something special had occurred. Producer Moya Doherty, composer Bill Whelan, and myself set about creating a stage show that could build on the thrill, the spectacle and the sheer creative energy of that first television appearance.

The challenge was not simply to achieve a working production. We wanted to open out the new vision of Irish dance, to have it share a stage with other forms of dance from throughout the world. We dreamed that by doing so, these dances would mingle and spark off each other so as to create a performance with its own identity. It would be a performance rooted in the folk memory and arts of the Irish people; yet fresh, unique and exciting, and accessible to people everywhere.

In Dublin in 1995 the first fully staged threatrical production of **Riverdance** met with an acclaim that was loud with the pride and pleasure of the Irish public. Then in turn, in London, the West End's first night applause made it clear that this show could and would travel outside Ireland to rapturous approval.

But could it go further? None of us will ever forget the first night in New York, when a glittering audience filled six thousand seats in Radio City Music Hall. In the tension that always precedes curtain-up, I looked across the rows of expectant faces of those six thousand, and wondered how they would react. Had we overreached ourselves? Could this show that had come from all our hearts really take another city and a different continent by storm? In the thunderous standing ovation that followed, we knew what the entertainment world now knows: that **Riverdance** had crossed all boundaries and taken its place as a performance that the whole theatre-going world would enjoy.

There are now three companies touring the world. These companies, named after Irish rivers – the Boyne, the Corrib and the Foyle – have become a kind of extended family, even a small village. The dancers, musicians and singers don't simply perform together; they travel the world together, looking after each other, sharing their energies and aspirations, pushing each other to new heights and to the highest of standards. I know that for the Irish dancers and all the other performers the thrill of the dancing itself is magnified by an inner pride. It is the pride that comes from knowing that they are bringing the dancing and music of their own countries, their own people, to the world at large.

From all of us involved in creating **Riverdance** there is that same pride. There is also a deep pleasure in finding between us and within us the different elements that have helped to weave this multifaceted performance. My own experience is that of having worked for three decades in directing television and stage performances of every kind. Bill Whelan's credits as a composer of music for theatre and television and as a record producer speak for themselves. Moya Doherty's wide-ranging talents in production and direction essentially brought **Riverdance** into being. These combined experiences produced a vision and a concept that were brought richly to life by innovative choreography, charismatic dancers and musicians, lighting a spark that has changed the presentation and perception of Irish music and dance forever. For all of us, **Riverdance** has become an extraordinary opportunity to create a showcase for the dancers and musicians who – finally and above all – bring the stage thunderously to life, night after remarkable night.

And that is the key. I know, from watching **Riverdance** in theatres and arenas across the world, that this moment of spectacle and uplifting energy is as fresh now as it was in that first performance in April 1994. We work hard and tirelessly to make it so. Because that moment, that freshness, is – finally – what drives us all onward each night as the music begins and the dancers step forward looking into the expectant faces filling the auditorium and knowing that for this audience, as for each audience before them, it is always first night.

'A triumph of pure spectacle, weaves a powerful spell
that can leave an audience breathless'
Toronto Sun, Canada

'unadulterated exhilaration, irresistibly joyful,
brilliantly contemporary, life affirming'
What's On, London, UK

'Fills the stage with passion and joy'
Asahi Newspaper, Japan

'close to 10,000 people applauded until their hands hurt'
Excelsior, Mexico

'One of the entertainment legends of our time'
The Belfast Newsletter, Northern Ireland

'...the original...the best'
The Irish Times, Ireland

'a hurricane you will never forget, you have to see it'
Bild Hamburg, Germany

'A whirlwind of music and dance, a radiant show'
Le Progrès, France

'The show is quite simply incredible'
The Washington Times, USA

'Triumphant! A perfect gem!'
New York Post, USA

THE HEART OF RIVERDANCE
BY JULIAN ERSKINE, SENIOR EXECUTIVE PRODUCER

As I set off from home early on the morning of 12th November 1994 in my Fiat Tipo to collect Michael Flatley and Jean Butler from their apartments to fly to London I had no idea that this was to be the first step of a long and exciting journey, that would take me around the world (several times) and that would take over my life completely for the following 15 years.

The reason we were going to London was to perform **Riverdance** at a private function in the Royal Albert Hall. This was to be the first live performance of the piece since Eurovision and also marked the start of the creative rehearsal period that would culminate with **Riverdance**, the show, opening in the Point Theatre the following February.

It has been an amazing 15 years, in fact amazing is too slight a word to describe that magical journey from that November morning through to this present day. Very few shows survive long past their opening nights, few are revived to see the light of day again and only a handful have made it past the 10 year mark, **Riverdance** is clearly one of those special shows that has those elusive magical ingredients.

The show has been through many incarnations as it has evolved over the years, especially during its first five years, but the one constant has been the heart of the show and for me the heart of **Riverdance** is pride. People who work on the show are proud of it and those who perform in it are doing so with pride as they nightly represent their culture and their heritage on stage.

I have also always believed that another of the reasons for the success of the show is the purity of its creation. Unlike so many shows, it did not come from a need to fill a gap in a schedule, or to fulfil a commission or to trade on someone else's successful idea, it came as an honest response to the enormous effect of that seven minute interval act in Eurovision and it was born out of an intense period of inspired and imaginative development by its creators, as they invented a new genre of show and a new type of entertainment. It was so fresh, so spirited and so young that it took people's breath away with its energy and its commitment.

It is that commitment that has allowed us to play in halls, theatres and arenas across the globe, from the 1,000 seats of the Gaiety Theatre in Dublin to the 11,000 seats in the National Auditorium in Mexico City, and everywhere the effect has been the same; **Riverdance** reaches out and touches everyone. Its universal appeal crosses geographical and cultural boundaries. I have seen audiences laugh and cry from Adelaide to Anchorage and inevitably they have all risen to their feet at the end to show their appreciation, and I always feel we have done our job well if members of the audience 'dance' their way out of the theatre after the show with smiles on their faces.

Well the Fiat Tipo is long gone, but the **Riverdance** journey continues. It's different today but in an important way it's still exactly the same. There have been changes and there have been the downs as well as the ups and many dancers, singers, musicians, crew and staff have passed through the show over the years. We don't travel with as many trucks as we used to and nowadays we might play 1 week in a city where we used play 2, but that's OK, that's just the passage of time.

Recently I visited the Boyne Company in Canada, I had not seen the show for a few weeks and as always I was looking forward to seeing it. What I did not expect was the wave of emotion that hit me as the lights went down and the music started and despite having seen it thousands of times it still moved me and made me so proud to be part of it, just as much as it did when I stood on the side of the stage in the Albert Hall all those years ago. •

HISTORY OF A PHENOMENON

Riverdance, The Eurovision Song Contest, 30th April, 1994.

Riverdance – The Show, Dublin Premiere, February 9th, 1995.

94

Riverdance opens in the Apollo Hammersmith, London, June 1995.

Riverdance opens in Radio City Music Hall, New York, March 1996.

By late 1996 there were two **Riverdance** touring companies established which were named after Irish rivers, the Lee and the Liffey.

The first non-English speaking audience experienced **Riverdance** in Oberhausen, Germany, in July 1997.

Bill Whelan with Quincy Jones

Bill Whelan was honoured with the 1997 Grammy Award for 'Best Musical Show Album' for his ***Riverdance*** CD. The album is a Certified Platinum Record in the US, Ireland and Australia and has sold over 2.5 million copies worldwide. In 1994 the single release went straight to No. 1 in the Irish charts and held that position for 18 weeks – a record only broken by Elton John's tribute to Princess Diana. In 1996 the ***Riverdance*** CD entered the Billboard World Music Chart at No. 1 and stayed in that position for 36 weeks.

A third touring **Riverdance** company, the Lagan was launched in Vancouver in 1998.

Riverdance travelled East for the first time in 1999 to perform to sell-out audiences in Tokyo and Osaka.

The **Riverdance** Flying Squad was established to perform at private, corporate and charity events as well as promotional events.

In 2000 the Liffey company brought **Riverdance** back to Dublin for 'The Homecoming'. On the 28th June 2001, **Riverdance** was hours away from opening in Madrid for the first time when the venue went up in flames. Almost the entire **Riverdance** production was destroyed. The Madrid dates were cancelled but the producers promised to be ready for the next tour, due to start exactly 2 months later in Germany. The show opened in Köln as promised. The audience welcomed the rebuilt production with rapturous applause.

A limited engagement was announced for Broadway in March 2000. **Riverdance** performed on Broadway at the Gershwin Theatre for 18 months until August 2001 when it closed after a hugely successful run.

During March 2002 the Lagan and Liffey companies celebrated the 5000th **Riverdance** performance with shows in San Francisco and Edinburgh, Scotland.

In June 2003 **Riverdance** performed at the opening ceremony of the 2003 Special Olympics World Summer Games in Dublin's Croke Park. The performance featured the longest ever **Riverdance** line, with over 100 dancers filling the vast stage before 80,000 audience members and games participants.

In October 2003 the Liffey company took **Riverdance** to China for the first time. The venue in Beijing was the Great Hall of the People.

Riverdance returned to Dublin with a new company, the Foyle, in 2004, performing in the Gaiety Theatre, Dublin. Building on the success of the Dublin show a second Irish venue, Killarney, was added in 2006.

In June 2007 **Riverdance** performed at the Wolf Trap Centre for the Performing Arts in Vienna, Virginia, USA, for a record breaking 10th time.

The 10th anniversary of **Riverdance** in 2005 was marked with a series of sell-out performances in Radio City Music Hall, NYC.

RIVERDANCE FACTS

In it's first fifteen years, since **Riverdance** began performances in Dublin 1995, the show has...

Played over 10,000 performances

Been seen live by over 22 million people in over 300 venues worldwide, throughout 32 countries, across 4 continents

Travelled 563,000 miles *(or to the moon and back!)*

Played to a global television audience of over 2 billion people

Sold over 3 million copies of the Grammy Award-winning CD

Sold over 10 million **Riverdance** videos and DVDs

And there have been...

900 Performers

14,000 Dance shoes used

12,000 Costumes worn

200,000 Gallons of water consumed

60,000 Gallons of Gatorade consumed

1,650,000 Show programmes sold

1,500 Flight cases used

12,000 Stage lighting bulbs used

40,000 Boxes of tissues used

16,250 Guitar, bass and fiddle strings replaced

284,000 T-shirts sold

35 Marriages between company members

20,000 Cumulative years of study in step-dancing by Irish Dancers

45,000 Rolls of self-grip tape used by company physiotherapists

15,000 Hours of rehearsals on tour

5,500,000 Pounds of dry ice used on stage

60,000 Pounds of chocolate consumed *(for energy!)* by the cast

1,000,000 Page views a month on **www.riverdance.com**

Jean Butler & Michael Flatley   Tara Barry & Michael Pat Gallagher

Joanne Doyle & Breandán de Gallaí   Jean Butler & Colin Dunne

Sinead McCafferty & Conor Hayes   Melissa Convery & Padraic Moyles

Zara Curtis & Joe Moriarty   Eileen Martin & Pat Roddy

Credits

Composer	Bill Whelan
Producer	Moya Doherty
Director	John McColgan
Senior Executive Producer for Riverdance	Julian Erskine
Set Design	Robert Ballagh
Lighting Design	Rupert Murray
Costume Design	Joan Bergin
Original costume designer for Riverdance The Show	Jen Kelly
Riverdance at Eurovision Song Contest costume design	Margaret Crosse
Sound Design	Michael O'Gorman
Projection Animation	Benjamin Pearcy
Projection Design	Chris Slingsby
Original Irish Dance Choreography	Michael Flatley
Additional Choreography	Mavis Ascott
	Jean Butler
	Colin Dunne
	Carol Leavy Joyce
	Andrei Kisselev
	Moscow Folk Ballet Company
	María Pagés
	Tarik Winston
Poetry	Theo Dorgan
Original Point Production Designer	Mary Morrow
Original Point Lighting Design	Andrew Leonard
Original Point Projection Design	Dick Straker
Original Riverdance Logo Design	Image Now Consultants
Riverdance Graphic Design	Zeus Design

110

Creative Team

Julian Erskine (Senior Executive Producer for **Riverdance**), Robert Ballagh (Set Design), Joan Bergin (Costume Design), Maurice Cassidy (International Promoter), Michael O'Gorman (Sound Design).

The Producers would like to give special acknowledgement to: Conor Sexton, RTE Commercial Enterprises Ltd, Paul McGuinness, Principle Management, Maurice Cassidy, Tommy Higgins

Rupert Murray (Lighting Design)
3rd February 1951 – 17th August 2006

Riverdance Cast 1994-2010

THE RIVERDANCE IRISH DANCERS
(PRINCIPALS AND TROUPE)

Caitlin Allen
Alejandro Arguelles
Craig Ashurst (PD)
Liam Ayres (PD)
Jessica Baffa
Paul Bailey
Patrick Barnett
Owen Barrington
Sarah Barry
Tara Barry (PD)
Dearbhail Bates
Orfhlaith Bates
Seán Beglan (PD)
Paula Bell
David Bellwood
Michael Belvitch
Gili Ben Ari
Meaghan Berne
Lisa Berry
Natalie Biggs
Bobbie Ann Boeing
Karen Bolton (PD)
Caroline Boyce
Donna Marie Boyle (PD)
Gavin Boyle
Lorna Bradley

Caroline Brennan
Martin Brennan (PD)
Stephen Brennan
Keith Brett
Claire Brett
Ciaron Brooks
Abigail Browne
Niamh Browne
Florian Bruillet
Michelle Buffini
Maria Buffini (PD)
Eugene Burke
Nina Burke
Siobhan Burke
Jean Butler (PD)
Maureen Byrne
Nicola Byrne (PD)
Rachel Byrne
Steven Byrne
Kelley Byrne
Emma Caden
Róisín Cahalan (PD)
Zephanias Caissie
Karl Callaghan
Mary Jo Cange
Gemma Cannon

Nora Cannon
John Carey
Doireann Carney
Gemma Carney
Ryan Carroll (U)
Sabrina Carty
Cara Casey (PD)
Darren Casey
Niamh Champion
Orla Clarke (PD)
Lisa Clarke
Aoife Clarke
Teresa Clarkson
Suzanne Cleary (PD)
Yzanne Cloonan
Shona Cobbe
Garrett Coleman
Odharnait Colley
Catherine Collins (PD)
Maureen Collins
Joey Comerford
Donal Conlan
Linda Conlan (U)
Margaret Conneely
Erin Connolly
Sean Connolly

PD – Principal Dancer
U – Understudy

Ciaran Connolly
Melissa Convery (PD)
Nora Corrigan (PD)
Caterina Coyne (PD)
Patrick Coyne
Breege Creaven
Maeve Croke
Aileen Cronin
Danielle Crosthwaite
Angela Crowley
Anne-Marie Cunningham
Daniel Cunningham
Fiona Cunningham
Fiona Cunningham
Isobel Cunningham
Joanne Cunningham
Andrea Curley
Kevin Curran
Noelle Curran
Sinead Curran
Zara Curtis (PD)
Paul Cusick
Christopher Daly
Brenda Daly
Erin Davidson
Breandan De Gallai (PD)
Benedict Devlin
Damian Doherty
Scott Doherty
Christina Dolzall
Aileen Donaghy
Michael Donegan
Michael Donnellan (U)

Maeve Donohoe
Terry Donovan
Kathleen Doohan
Brendan Dorris (PD)
Marty Dowds (PD)
Deirdre Dowling
Claire Doyle
Joanne Doyle (PD)
Lindsay Doyle
Shannon Doyle
Aisling Drennan
Jacqueline Duggan
Liam Duggan
Colin Dunne (PD)
Lindsay Ellis
Emily Endean
Niall Ennis
Michael Eustace (PD)
Niamh Eustace
Mairead Joanne Evans
Derek Fahy
Anthony Fallon (PD)
Jillian Farmer
Attracta Farrell
Dearbhla Fay
Seamus Fearon
Maeve Fearon
Ciara Fenlon
Anthony Ferguson
Patricia Finnegan
Katie Flannery
Michael Flatley (PD)
Eddie Flynn

Sean Flynn
Maryanne Fogarty
Kristyn Fontanella
JoEllen Forsyth
Alan Fox
Sean Fox
Bobby Fox
Barry John Gallagher
Catherine Ann Gallagher
Clare Gallagher
George Bernard Gallagher
Lorraine Gallagher
Michael Pat Gallagher (PD)
Tracey Gallagher
Fiona Gallagher (Derry)
Fiona Gallagher (Donegal)
Rachel Galligan
Michael Galvin
Siobhan Gargan
Nicholas Gayeski
Oliver Gemoli
Yvonne Gibson
Stephen Gillespie
Susan Ginnety (PD)
Mark Gorman
Paula Goulding (U)
Deirdre Goulding
Freda Gray
Sinead Greene (PD)
Orla Griffin
John Grimes
John Guerin
Lori Hall

Karen Halley
Deirdre Hamilton (PD)
Fiona Hand
Katie Hands
Joel Hanna
Kieran Hardiman
Peter Harding (U)
Liam Harney (PD)
Fiona Harold
Rachael Harris
Sarah Harris (U)
Christina Havlin (PD)
Taka Hayashi
Bridgit Hayden
Conor Hayes (PD)
Eileen Healy
Gary Healy
Jennifer Healy
Charlene Hegarty
Tara Hegarty
Craig Henderson
Enda Heneghan
Patricia Henry
James Hester
Carol Hetherington
Lisa Hetherington
Zoe Heynes
Lexa Hickey
Conor Holmes
Miceal Hopkins
Sarah Hopkins
Kevin Horton
Kerry Houston

PD – Principal Dancer
U – Understudy

Donnacha Howard (U)
Maria Hueston
Catherine Hughes
Kellie Hughes
Kerry Hutchinson
Jason Hynan
Theresa Ierardi
Kathy Irvine
Nicola Irvine
Ciara-lee Jenkinson
David Johnston
William Kanaly
Kathleen Keady
Orla Keane
Gearóid Keane
Seán Keane
Edel Kearney
James Keating
Kellie Keegan
Orla Keeler
Sean Kelliher (PD)
Ryan Kelly
Shane Kelly
Alan Kenefick (PD)
Ciara Kennedy (U)
Mairead Kennedy
Fiona Kidd
Aidan Kilcoyne
Damian Kirk
Tim Kochka
Ilkka Kuosmanen
Siobhán Lambert (U)

Grace Lavelle
Carol Leavy-Joyce
Dearbhla Lennon (PD)
Nicola Leonard
Deborah Lewsley
Sinéad Lightley
Tara Little
Sabrina Long
Lisa Loran
Dara Loughrey
Meghan Lucey
Yvonne Lynch
Gillian Madders
Ciaran Maguire
Darren Maguire (U)
Ellie Maguire
Katie Maguire
Michael Maguire
Yvonne Mahady
Conor Maher
Pamela Maher
Alana Mallon (PD)
Marcus Maloney
Sarah Manning
Siobhán Manson (PD)
Eileen Martin (PD)
Matt Martin
Craig Mason
Mairead Masuda (PD)
Tokiko Masuda
Maura McArdle
Stephen McAteer

Shane McAvinchey
Fiona McCabe
Sinéad McCafferty (PD)
Ryan McCaffrey (PD)
Brendan McCarron
Ryan McCarthy
Sorcha McCaul
Claire McCole
Mark McCole
Eireann McCormack
Kevin McCormack (U)
Ronan McCormack
Alanna McCrudden
Aoife McDarby
Niamh McDarby
Deirdre McDonnell (PD)
Emily McDonnell
Debbie McGahan
Caroline McGarrell
Dervla McGee
Mary McGeough
Ciara McGillan (PD)
Holly McGlinchey
Sarah McGowan
Christina McGrath
Katie McGrath
Declan McHale
Nicole McKeever
Joanne McKenna (U)
Michelle McKitterick
Sinead McLaughlin
Gregory McMahon

Paula McManus
Claire McManus
Jason McMorrow
Jonathan McMorrow
Claire McNelis
Yvonne McNelis
Paula McNelis
Oisín McQuoid
Siobhán McSharry
Jemma McSloy
Aisling McVeigh
Laura Minogue
Susannah Moffitt
David Moore (PD)
Derek Moran
Cal Moran
Jennifer Moriarty
Joe Moriarty (PD)
Neil Morrison
Padraic Moyles (PD)
Brian Mullane
Laura Mulligan
Niall Mulligan
Laura Mulqueen
Gerard Mulrey
Rachel Mulvihill
Damian Murphy
Lisa Murphy
Eimear Murphy
Lorcan Murphy
Louise Murphy
Elaine Murphy-Laps

114

PD – Principal Dancer
U – Understudy

Sarah Murray
Kelly Nagan
Chris Naish
Kathleen Natter (PD)
Dawn Nestor
Arlene Ní Bhaoill (U)
Mairead Ní Bhriain
Riona Ní Fhrighil
Dara Ní She
Caitlin Nic Gabhann
Sam Nicholas
Richard Nicholl
Andrew Nolan
Cheryl Nolan
Damien Noone
Linda Nurney
Arlene O'Brien
Carla O'Brien (PD)
Catherine O'Brien
Derval O'Brien
Seán O'Brien
Aoibheann O'Brien
Niamh O'Brien
Jennifer O'Connell
Kyle O'Connor
Niamh O'Connor
Oriel O'Dwyer
Emer O'Grady
David O'Hanlon
John O'Hara
Deborah O'Keeffe
Katrina O'Leary

Mark O'Loughlin
Damian O'Neill
Jason O'Neill
Andrew O'Reilly
Deirdre O'Reilly
Pauline O'Reilly
Gerard O'Reilly
Jason Oremus (PD)
Shannon O'Riordan
Amy O'Rourke
Jordan Osborne
Colm O'Se (U)
Cormac O'Se
Suzanne O'Sullivan
Conor Peden
Erin Pender
Gary Pender
Martin Percival
Scott Porter (U)
Ursula Quigley
Edel Quin
Erin Quinn
Paddy Quinn
Joan Rafter (U)
Lucia Rafter
Nicole Rankin
Julie Regan (U)
Katie Regan
Sean Regan
Jemma Reid
Geraldine Reidy
Anne Reilly

Margaret Revis
Danielle Rock
Pat Roddy (PD)
Niamh Roddy (PD)
Áine Rooney
Aislinn Ryan (PD)
Ann Ryan
Aoife Ryan
Colin Ryan
Doireann Ryan
Edel Ryan
Jennifer Ryan
Joanne Ryan
Justin Ryan
Lisa Ryan
Sheila Ryan
Gwenno Saunders
Alan Scariff (PD)
Rosemarie Schade
Edward Searle
Anthony Sharkey (PD)
Jacintha Sharpe
Jennifer Sharpe
Ryan Sheridan
Ronan Sherlock
Kevin Sherry
Amy Siegel
Glen Simpson (U)
Ronan Slevin
David Smith
Conor Smith
Lauren Smyth

Kelly Stephens
Eulalia Stewart
Martina Stewart
Alex Strange
Brian Swanton
Tracey Taaffe
Orfhlaith Taylor
Ross Thompson
Arlene Toal
Colin Toland
Anne Toner
Daniel Triggle
Chloey Turner
Claire Usher
JR Vancheri
Ronan Wall
Eithne Walls
Raymond Walls
Regina Walsh
Justin Walsh
Francis Ward
Leanda Ward
Eileen Westernacher
Lynsey Wilkinson
Ashley Wilkinson
Margaret Williams
Nicole Williams
Jillian Winke
Stephanie Wright
Nicholas Yenson

PD – Principal Dancer
U – Understudy

THE RIVERDANCE MUSICIANS

Kennedy Aitchison (MD)
Mark Alfred
Nicky Bailey
Conor Barry
Ivan Barvich
Matt Bashford
Stephen Benson
Paul Booth
Máire Breathnach
Fran Breen
Lloyd Byrne
Stuart Calvert (MD)
Nollaig Casey
Robbie Casserly
Brian Connor (MD)
Zoe Conway
Ewan Cowley
Joe Csibi (MD)
Luke Daniels
Matt Darriau
Nigel Davey
Fionán de Barra
Dan Dorrance
Mark Dougherty (MD)
David Downes (MD)
Brendan Doyle
Zac Drummond
Patrick Dunne (MD)
Noel Eccles (MD)
Kenneth Edge
Éilís Egan

Chris Eminizer
Máirín Fahy
Niamh Fahy
Ray Fean
Mark Fineberg
Eamonn Galldubh
Colm Gannon
Carl Geraghty
Rob Geraghty
Ivan Gilliland
Ivan Goff
Carolyn Goodwin
Kevin Hanafin
Robbie Harris
Tommy Hayes
David Hayes (MD)
Noel Heraty
Jim Higgins
Stephen Hogan
John Hogan
Steve Holloway
Eileen Ivers
Sarah James
Don Johnson
Julian Kelly (MD)
Alan Kelly
Toby Kelly (MD)
Alexis MacIsaac
Pat Mangan
David Mann
Patrick Martin

Tommy Martin
Maria Mason
Declan Masterson (MD)
Martin McCormack
Gemma McCrisken
Johnny McDonagh
David McGauran
John McSherry
Mel Mercier
Maria Millar
Des Moore
Paul Moore (MD)
Paul Moran
Frankie Mulcahy
Darragh Murphy
Donal Murphy
Eoghan Neff
Flaithrí Neff
Aoife Ní Bhriain
Niamh Ní Charra
Albert Niland
Tomas Ó'Briain
Brian O'Brien
John O'Brien
Mick O'Brien
Máirtín O'Connor
Martin O'Hare
Colm O'Foghlu (MD)
Athena O'Loughlin
Eoghan O'Neill (MD)
Brendan O'Sullivan

Nikola Parov
Peyo Peev
Georgi Petrov
Robin Pitre
Amy Platt
Brendan Power
Damien Quinn
Andrew Reilly
Martin C. Reilly
Marie Reilly
Desmond Reynolds
Guy Rickarby (MD)
Rafael Riqueni
Nicky Scott
Danny Sheridan
Mikie Smyth
Theodosii Spassov-Iordanov
Davy Spillane
Tony Steele
Cathal Synnott (MD)
Derrick Tallon
Kelvin Thomson (MD)
Cillian Vallely
Kevin Walsh (MD)
David Weiss
John Whelan
Brian Whelan
Pete Whinnett
Dave Whyte •

MD – Musical Director

118

ANÚNA AND THE RIVERDANCE SINGERS
(SOLOISTS AND CHOIR MEMBERS)

Robert Archibald
Catherine Bamford
Miriam Blennerhasset
Richard Boyle
Denise Brennan
Brenda Brooks
Anne Buckley
Sarah Burgess
Derek Byrne
Eoin Cannon
Amy Carrick
Paul Carroll
Jonathan Carter
Sara Clancy
David Clarke
Derek Collins
Paddy Connolly
Aidan Conway
Sean Cooper
Lorraine Cotter
Morgan Crowley
Jennifer Curran
Tony Davoren
Esther Dee
Kira Deegan
Róisín Dempsey
Brian Dunphy
Julian Edwards
Marc Ellery

Kathryn Else
Susan Facer
Joanna Fagan
Caitriona Fallon
Elizabeth Farnum
Mark Fennell
Stephen Flanagan
Denise Flynn
Liz Foster
Brioni Gallagher
Fionnuala Gill
Julie Gillan
Hayley Griffiths
Gary Haas
Caron Hannigan
Peter Harney
Gary Harpur
Kate Harvey
Laine Henderson
Joanna Higgins
Lynn Hilary
Alison Hill
Andrew Holden
Darren Holden
Patrick Hughes
Morgan James
Tim Jay
Pam Jolley
Helen Kelly

Lisa Kelly
Colette Kidney
Elizabeth Knowles
George Komsky
Máire Lang
Emer Lang
Kay Lynch
Jackie Mahon
Bernadette Mahony
John Matthews
Niamh McCormack
Catriona McEleney
Ian McGlynn
John McGlynn
Tom McGlynn
Meara McIntyre
Ian McLarnon
Katie McMahon
Conor Mellon
John Molloy
Kendal Mooney
Jeremy Morgan
Simon Morgan
Máire Mullarkey
Ann Myler
Ciaran Nagle
Caroline Newman
Mairéad Ní Fhaoláin
Maeve Ní Mhaolchatha

Lorraine Nolan
Tara O'Beirne
Robert O'Connor
Ann O'Kane
Denise O'Kane
Curtis Olds
Kenneth O'Regan
Tony O'Sullivan
Avril O'Toole
Gareth Patterson
Cary Posavitz
Amy Rivard
Michael Sands
James Sasser
Suzanne Savage
Mary Sexton
Sherry Steele
Naoise Stuart-Kelly
Ben Stubbs
Róisín Sullivan
Jessica Summers
Colette Todd
Fiona Wight
Jeannie Wyse
Laura Yanez ⦁

THE RIVERDANCE FLAMENCO SOLOISTS

Carmen Armengou
Nuria Brisa
Marina Claudio Manso
Yolanda González Sobrado
Almudena Hernández Martínez
Marta Jiménez Luis
Arantxa Jurado
Rosa Manzano Jiménez
Marita Martínez-Rey
Rebeca Mateos Morante
Rocio Montoya
María Pagés
Nelida Tirado ●

THE MOISEYEV DANCE COMPANY AND
THE MOSCOW FOLK BALLET COMPANY

Ilia Andreev
Alexander Belov
Denis Berko
Ekaterina Boroditskaya
Denis Boroditski
Roman Brovkin
Anna Brovkina
Sergey Bukreev
Leonila Buldakova
Andriy Buluy
Timur Chernov
Andrij Cybyk
Elena Demianenko
Natalia Ejova
Carmella Gallace
Elena Grinko
Sergey Iakubov
Lilia Ialalova
Marina Iatsevich
Iouri Jivoglotov
Igor Karpenko
Natalia Kartavtseva
Andrei Kisselev
Ioulia Koriaguina
Svetlana Kossourokova
Dmitry Krivenko
Olena Krutsenko
Alexey Kuksa

Ruslan Kurikba
Valentina Kvasova
Yulia Lykuanova
Ganna Makarova
Nelli Maksimovitch
Svetlana Malinina
Sadagyul Mamedova
Liubov Marchukova
Irina Maslennikova
Maria Minakova
Tatiana Nedostup
Mikhail Nesterenko
Kirill Nikitin
Ilia Pankratov
Eduard Resnik
Natia Rtveliashvili
Alexey Rybalkin
Ekaterina Shaymratova
Elena Shibaeva
Yury Shishkin
Olga Shpitalnaya
Natalia Sidorova
Olga Siracheva
Dmitry Smyslov
Alexei Sorokin
Irina Soukhinina
Evgeniya Starodubova
Ilia Streltsov

Alexey Sukharev
Marina Taranda
Yevgeni Tatyankin
Natalia Tomilina
Margarita Trotsenko
Yury Ustyugov
Oleg Vasiliev
Vitaly Verterich
Yana Volkova
Danila Vyazovikin
Vatcheslav Yankovskiy
Alexey Zamakhaev
Yulia Zhukova •

THE RIVERDANCE TAPPERS

Charon Aldredge
Brill Barrett
Ronald Cadet Bastine
Jason E. Bernard
Troy Blackwell Cook
Robet Burden
Karen Callaway-Williams
Michael Clorey
DeJuan Collins
Lathaniel Cooper
Rogelio Douglas
Martin Dumas III
Walter "Sundance" Freeman
Jelly Germaine
Parker Hall
Toby Harris
Leon Hazelwood
Rolondas Hendricks
Channing Holmes
Nick Holmes
Corey Hutchins
Kelly Isaac
Waylon Jacobs
Dexter Jones
Junior Laniyan
Parris Mann
Richard O'Neal
Lee Payne
Marcel Peneux

Rohan Pinnock-Hamilton
Van "The Man" Porter
Robert Reed
Donnell Russell
Johnathan Scott
Sean Scott
Jimmy Tate
Arthur Taylor
Aaron Tolson
Herbin Van Cayseele
Joseph Wiggan
Tarik Winston
DeAndre Lewis Wolf
Danny Wooten •

THE RIVERDANCE BASS BARITONE SOLOISTS

Michel Bell
Ralph Cato
David Aron Damane
Michael Danso
Kevin Deas
Charles Gray
Mark Anthony Hall
Miritana Hughes
Garth Jacobs
Darrin Lamont-Byrd
Richard McCowen

Joseph Noble
Robert Parks
Walter Reynolds
Ronald Samm
Michael Samuels
Raphael Darryl Sligh
Anton Stephans
Ivan Thomas
Johannes Van Duisburg
Kirk Walker •

THE RIVERDANCE ONSTAGE DRUMMERS

Darren Andrews
Steve Arthur
Ara Babajian
Mark Champion
Abe Doron
Derek Doyle
Eamon Ellams
Jarod Gibson
Shaunagh Ginty
Gary Grant
Kevin McHugh
Colin McNamara

Ian McTigue
David Moran
Alistair Morris
Johnny Norton
Aran O'Malley
Vinnie Ozborne
Matt Parker
Rod Shiels
Darren Smith
David Tilly
Gareth Winstone •

THE RIVERDANCE FEATURED SOLOISTS

Brian Kennedy
Tsidii Le Loka
Anna Ross
Aine Ui Cheallaigh •

THE DELIVERANCE ENSEMBLE CHOIR
(ORIGINAL PRODUCTION AT THE POINT THEATRE, DUBLIN)

James Bignon
Christy Clarke
Chris Hagan
Raymond Hicks
Roberta Higgs
Alunda Marks
Philip McClian
Cheryl Sparks
Selena Swint
Jedidiah Williams •

THE AMANZI CHOIR
(RIVERDANCE ON BROADWAY)

Ntombikhona Dlamini
Vukani Dlamini
Rosena Hill
Fana Kekana
Cassie Kekana
Ntombifuthi Pamela Mhlongo
Francina Moliehi Mokubetsi
Keneilwe Margaret Motsage
Isaac Mthethwa
Andile Selby Ndelbele
Mbuso Dick Shange •

Over the years a host of celebrities have come to see Riverdance. Top: Gabriel Byrne, Bill Clinton and John McColgan. Bottom left: Moya Doherty, Brian Kennedy and Bill Whelan check out Broadway reviews. Bottom right: President Mary McAleese and her husband, Martin at Riverdance, Beijng, China. Opposite – Top: Niamh Eustace and Conor McCarthy with the Irish Olympic Boxing Team, Beijing, China. Bottom: Cast and crew of Riverdance with the Irish Boxing Team and the Irish Ambassador Declan Kelleher at the Riverdance Opening Night of the Olympics, Beijing, China, 2008.

Left – top: Moya Doherty and Liam Neeson.
Bottom: Her Imperial Majesty, The Empress of Japan with the Irish Ambassador, Brendan Scanlon. Tokyo, 2008.

Right – top: Mary McAleese China, 2008. Middle: Flying Squad in Kilmainham with Chinese Ambassador & Bertie Ahern.
Bottom: Ted Kennedy Jr, Jean Kennedy Smith and Moya Doherty.

Opposite: Bill Whelan, Moya Doherty, Gene Wilder.

PHOTOGRAPHY CREDITS

Copyright Abhann Productions
Pages 90, 96 *(lower right)*, 97 *(lower left)*,
111 *(lower)*, 116/117, 126 *(lower left)*

Ben Asen
Page 96 *(top)*

T.L. Boston
Page 94 *(lower left)*

Barbara Corsico
Page 78 *(left)*

Anthony Crickmay
Page 7

Hugo Glendinning
Pages 23, 24 *(left)*, 26, 65

Jack Hartin Photography
Pages 9/10, 12/13, 17, 18/19, 20, 21, 22 *(left)*,
24 *(right)*, 25, 27, 32, 33, 34, 35, 36, 37, 38, 39, 40,
41, 42, 43, 44, 48, 49, 51, 52, 53, 54 *(top)*, 56, 57,
58/59, 60, 61, 62, 63, 64 *(left)*, 66, 67 *(top)*, 68, 69,
70, 71, 72, 73, 74, 75, 76, 77, 79, 80, 81, 82, 83,
89, 101 *(lower)*, 109 *(top and lower left)*, 117, 132/133

Chris Hill
Pages 4, 93, 94 *(top)*, 95, 108 *(top left and lower right)*

Mick Hutson
Pages 45, 105 *(lower right)*

Darren Kinsella
Page 111 *(group photo)*

Tom Lawlor
Page 94 *(right)*

Maxwell Photo Agency
Page 126 *(lower right)*, 128 *(top right and middle right)*

Michael Le Poer Trench
Page 108 *(lower left)*

Robert Llewellyn
Page 104 *(top)*

Joan Marcus
Pages 7, 54 *(lower)*, 55 *(lower)*, 67 *(lower)*, 84,
85, 95 *(lower 2 photos)*, 97 *(top and right))*, 98, 99,
105 *(top and lower left)*, 108 *(top right)*, 109 *(lower right)*,
121

Jim McCann
Page 15

Frank Miller
Page 29

Richard Nobel
Pages 16, 17

Kyran O'Brien
Pages 28, 55 *(top)*, 100, 102, 103

Riverdance Cast & Crew
Pages 101 *(top)*, 127

RTE Stills Library
Page 92 *(Eurovision Song Contest)*

Anita and Steve Shevett
Pages 14, 104 *(lower)*, 128 *(top left and lower right)*,
129

PRESS AND MEDIA ENQUIRIES

North America

Merle Frimark
North American Press/Marketing Representative
Merle Frimark Associates
1133 Broadway, Suite 1207
New York, NY 10010
Tel: 212-819-1133
Fax: 212-819-9898
E-mail: merle@merlefrimarkpr.com

Ireland and Rest of World

Gerry Lundberg Public Relations
24 South Frederick Street
Dublin 2
Ireland
Tel: + 353 1 679 8476
E-mail: glundpr@iol.ie

WWW.RIVERDANCE.COM